T0157357

THE GUIDE FOR FRONTLINE SUPERVISORS (AND THEIR BOSSES)

Tim Hewitt, Retired President and COO
and
Tom Zabor, retired VP of HR and Labor Relations

authorHOUSE®

AuthorHouse™
1663 Liberty Drive
Bloomington, IN 47403
www.authorhouse.com
Phone: 1-800-839-8640

© 2011. Tim Hewitt - Tom Zabor. All rights reserved

No part of this book may be reproduced, stored in a retrieval system, or transmitted by any means without the written permission of the author.

First published by AuthorHouse   7/14/2011

ISBN: 978-1-4634-0170-2 (sc)
ISBN: 978-1-4634-0169-6 (hc)
ISBN: 978-1-4634-0168-9 (e)

Library of Congress Control Number: 2011907389

Printed in the United States of America

Any people depicted in stock imagery provided by Thinkstock are models, and such images are being used for illustrative purposes only. Certain stock imagery © Thinkstock.

This book is printed on acid-free paper.

Because of the dynamic nature of the Internet, any web addresses or links contained in this book may have changed since publication and may no longer be valid. The views expressed in this work are solely those of the author and do not necessarily reflect the views of the publisher, and the publisher hereby disclaims any responsibility for them.

SU'PER VI'SOR One who oversees or directs the work of others.

According to the 1935 National Labor Relations Act, Section 2 (11):

The term "supervisor" means any individual having authority, in the interest of the employer, to hire, transfer, suspend, lay off, recall, promote, discharge, assign, reward, or discipline other employees, or responsibly to direct them, or to adjust their grievances, or effectively to recommend such action, if in connection with the foregoing the exercise of such authority is not of a merely routine or clerical nature, but requires the use of independent judgment.

Authors' note: An individual generally needs to satisfy only one of the above "employer interests" in order to qualify as a supervisor under the NLRA.

Contents

PREFACE

The inspiration for this book came to us at a bar, over drinks with the union leadership from our last place of joint employment. The union leaders had invited us to join them to celebrate Tom's retirement and Tim's promotion to another corporate position. The authors had worked together for over twenty years with other unions in other companies and had similarly celebrated other events with union leaderships.

The get-together was enjoyable as we recounted events of the past five years of working together in a dynamic environment of business transitions. High points and low points of collective bargaining and contract administration were reviewed. At one point a member of the union's Executive Committee told us that the two of us should write a book. In his opinion and the opinion of the other union members, our approach to dealing with employees, both union and nonunion, was honest, unique, and effective.

We had already planned to establish a consulting partnership, and we immediately felt that a book could be an excellent introduction to potential clients—while at the same time memorializing some of the unique successes we had achieved in our careers.

We discussed the idea, and we both agreed that a useful book, incorporating our experiences, could be best written from the perspective of the first line supervisor, the "credible messenger" that we had found over the years to be so vital in dealing with the employees of any organization. We reviewed our idea with a number of company leaders and human resource professionals, and they all strongly agreed that such a book was certainly needed in their organizations, many calling it "THE priority."

As we began to write, we knew that the link between the successes of any frontline supervisor and company leadership was too significant to ignore. The book has a primary focus on the frontline supervisor; we have tried, therefore, to clarify the absolute need of leadership communications, direction, and support of the frontline supervisor.

We also decided to avoid an academic approach and wrote in such a way as to practically summarize our experiences—what turned out to be a "toolbox" approach supervisors (and company leadership) can use as they encounter the different aspects and challenges of doing their jobs. Each chapter topic has been individually selected as dealing with an important ingredient, a tool, that we have learned (sometimes by trial and error) and that every supervisor should know.

Chapters have been introduced with hypothetical situations and questions that a supervisor might consider as new chapters begin. These introductions are there as "preparations" to generate some thought, and each individual supervisor should have other useful questions relevant to their own situation.

Finally, there are some basic concepts that we feel are imbedded in the book but need to be emphasized in dealing with this profession—and art—of supervision. One is quality. Although there are hundreds of books written about quality, it's our belief that the concept of quality can best be described as "doing the right thing, the correct way, the first time and each time." Obviously this is easier said than done but, with leadership support, efforts at continuous improvement should be a goal.

We have found also that most successful companies "invest" in their employees, in most cases by employee training and development. But we have found that companies that focus on a realistic employee evaluation process also can reap huge benefits.

This book was written to apply to most organizations and to all of its employees. The book is not pro-union or pro-management but has been written to objectively improve a company's business success through its people—via the frontline supervisor. While recognizing that company employee handbooks and collective bargaining agreements create unique business environments and cultures, we believe that this book in a simple way spells out concepts that, if executed, will improve your business success.

Tom Zabor and Tim Hewitt
Indianapolis, May 2011

INTRODUCTION

1. This handbook is intended as a practical "real life" guide to help organizations and their "frontline" supervisor level of management (the FLS). It is not a catchall, know-all textbook, but a sharing of what we have learned that works. We have tried to capture what, amid a sea of consultants and published books, has worked for us.

2. The marketplace seems to need this type of book. Our economy will grow as it always has, with small to medium-sized companies leading the way, and with a continuing need for people new to supervision. This book is written for them (and for company senior leadership).

3. People are a very important asset of any organization. Invest in them, trust them, listen to them, and communicate with them, and they will *want* to contribute to your business success.

4. Your employees need to know how your organization is making (and spending) money, and they need to understand the "business of your business."

5. The FLS's relationship with his or her own employees is a critical component of business success. This book is written more for the FLS, but the concepts can apply to any supervisor at any level. What the FLS and his or her team do together on a daily basis will drive your business success.

6. If the FLS does not understand the business or the business climate, neither will their employees.

7. An organization's senior management plays the key role in setting the stage for planning, communicating, guiding, measuring, and evaluating the success of the business. An organization's mission, vision, values, goals, objectives, and supporting business

processes (The "value and performance model"—V&P) need to be linked from top to bottom of the organization in a feedback loop in order to allow the FLS and other employees to know enough to help the organization succeed. This V&P model builds the organization's social and operating culture. It would be difficult for an organization to achieve optimum business success if there are inconsistencies in the alignment and execution of the V&P model.

8. Training and communication are essential in this loop, and it must be sponsored, supported, and reinforced by all senior management.

9. The FLS can use this book as a basis for a "contract for engagement" with employees. You share expectations with them, and they produce for you. (See Chapter 12 for an example.)

10. Quality is a concept all its own. There are hundreds of books written about quality. It is our belief that quality can best be defined as "doing the right thing, the correct way, each time." Obviously this is easier said than done, but certainly if leadership supports supervision's efforts to work with the employees doing the various tasks, quality will improve. And continuous improvement needs to be one of the company's annual goals. The concepts of quality and continuous improvement are in the same category as safety. Quality and continuous improvement need to be imbedded in the culture of the company as everyone's responsibility.

11. In many organizations, employees represent the largest costs to the business. Consequently, employers need to invest in all of their employees to make them more productive (and cost effective). The obvious employee investment is in training. But we have found that employers that develop and focus on an employee evaluation process reap huge benefits. This employee evaluation process will drive your training programs and your succession planning process.

12. The basic concept of execution is crucial to an organization's success. If you develop a business plan but don't execute, your results will likely be suboptimal. If you invest dollars in training for your employees but don't reinforce the training, those dollars will

be wasted. All of this seems simple enough, but in our experience most companies don't execute.

13. This book is intended as a summary/guide of topics that can be taught internally in any organization. The secret—if there is one—is to adopt a foundation philosophy of consistently communicating the "business of your business," linking all levels up and down the organization on a regular basis, emphasizing what your organization promises and expects.

Tips: **There's nothing new here, no rocket science—just basic common business sense tempered by our over eighty years of combined operating and human resources experience. It's basically about dealing effectively with people, the KEY to the FLS job.**

(We also believe strongly in the involvement of the FLS in the debates regarding the development of the organization's V&P Model—in order to assure alignment and execution of the business plans.)

Chapter 1

THE ROLE OF THE FRONTLINE SUPERVISOR

In Chapter one we provide a summary of the high level concepts that enable an employer and its Frontline Supervisors to understand the "balance" of this book and how the specific Tools we provide help the employer and supervisor succeed.

1. The execution of an organization's day-to-day operations is the primary responsibility of the frontline supervisor (FLS). Senior management has given that responsibility to the FLS. To a large extent, the level of an organization's long-term success relies on the effective execution of daily operations by the FLS. If the FLS can be relied on to effectively run daily operations, the rest of senior management can then focus their attention on longer term and more strategic business issues such as business development, acquisitions, market and technical research, and employee growth and development programs.

It seems obvious that the FLS plays a major role in an organization's success. Then why do many organizations struggle with daily operations and the relationship between senior management and the FLS? We believe one reason for this struggle is an absence in the business world of any effective tools that link senior management with the FLS. Senior management always has the best intentions, but as they face market challenges on a daily basis there is simply not enough time or any effective tools to address the linkage between senior management and the FLS.

The primary purpose of this book is to provide the tools that can make any organization more successful by linking all levels of the enterprise.

2. The FLS comes into her business role initially from a foreign perspective from the rest of management. In many cases, the FLS is selected for the position from the nonmanagement group because she is good at the work and probably shows some initiative. But she has very little or no supervisory experience. Frequently the FLS is placed into a situation where she is expected to supervise her old team. At best this is a very tricky situation for everyone. It should be avoided if at all possible until appropriate training is provided. The promoted individual needs to be prepared for this career change.

At the start, the FLS has one foot in the new world and one foot in the old world. She is neither "fish nor fowl." Without immediate and appropriate training, the new FLS will struggle and possibly fail. The failure of an FLS normally negatively impacts the business in myriad ways, such as lost profits, poor customer service, and poor employee relations—longer term, even lost customers.

In this book we intend to define the tools an organization can employ to assist in the effective transformation of an FLS. We want to explore some of the individual tools and concepts that will help make a new FLS more effective in her job.

3. The new FLS must quickly realize that he or she is now part of management. Their daily routine and job responsibilities will likely be drastically different than before they became an FLS.

4. While it is always desirable for all employees to feel like they are part of a larger team, the FLS will likely feel this in a profound way. The FLS will likely be a part of a group of supervisors that are not only linked by common goals and objectives but also linked by operations. The output of each department will impact the output of the other departments. The FLS must embrace the concept/reality that she is now part of a larger team—each member relying on the other.

5. Planning will be a big part of the FLS job duties. In addition to supervising day-to-day departmental operations, the FLS will need to set aside time to plan departmental job activities, prepare and execute employee performance appraisals of some type, budget,

forecast and prepare periodic management reports, communicate to employees the company news on a regular basis, and the list goes on. Developing effective time management skills is a must for everyone in management but especially for the FLS. This is the type of basic training that management should make available to everyone in management. By the way, being able to delegate certain job duties can be an effective time management tool, although this may be difficult for most. (Who's available to delegate to?)

6. The FLS must remember her primary allegiance is to the organization, and in most companies this usually means a responsibility to her boss and to her direct reports. Unfortunately, in many companies there is the element of politics. In our experience the best way to avoid or manage the politics is to communicate frequently, openly when appropriate, and honestly. And always remember who your boss is.

7. The FLS must be responsible for her own continued development and learning. This development and learning goes beyond company-sponsored training. The FLS needs to find opportunities to learn more about the overall business operation. Those opportunities may present themselves in less formal ways such as a discussion with a manager from another part of the business at lunch, a coffee break, or at the "water cooler." More formal opportunities may present themselves as well in the form of a division-wide or company-wide management meeting. Not only will understanding the big picture and how all of the "pieces" fit together in the running of the business help the FLS in supervising her department for success, it will give her knowledge that will improve her own worth to the company.

8. Finally, senior management's role is to create the overall environment that promotes the growth and success of the FLS. The role of the FLS in driving the organization's success cannot be ignored or overstated. In our experience it matters not what talent level the senior management team is or the value of the product, the organization's success will be diminished if the FLS cannot do her job effectively.

Notes

_____

_____

_____

_____

_____

_____

_____

_____

_____

_____

_____

_____

_____

_____

_____

_____

_____

_____

_____

_____

_____

Notes

_____

_____

_____

_____

_____

_____

_____

_____

_____

_____

_____

_____

_____

_____

_____

_____

_____

_____

_____

Chapter 2
THE BUSINESS OF YOUR BUSINESS

The Situation

Jim O'Brian is employed by a midsized manufacturing company, Acme Manufacturing, maker of plastic kitchen products and utensils.

Jim has worked for Acme for ten years as an electrician, having been hired soon after he completed a post-high-school apprenticeship program with a local union. Jim had a very good attendance record for Acme and became well liked by the management organization because of his "can-do" attitude and friendliness with most of the company's 125 employees. He accepted a promotion to a frontline supervisory position about one year ago.

Jim was relatively comfortable in his old electrician job. He liked his boss, and he liked the work he was doing—repairing electrical systems on Acme's manufacturing equipment. Acme's equipment was older and established, with few "state of the art" complications, and their processes had remained relatively stable during Jim's employment. He knew his job and was comfortable with it. He did what his boss assigned to him and didn't think much about the job or his employer once he left work every day.

Jim was now, after the promotion, feeling "out of his comfort zone" and was having second thoughts about why exactly he had taken the promotion to supervisor. He was now directly supervising twenty employees in a production assembly department, a far cry from his electrician's job. He knew the capabilities of the equipment being used in his department and knew his twenty employees, having bowled with many of them and having repaired the equipment most of them used over the years, but something was missing.

Jim had taken the job willingly because of the salary increase he was offered, the new career potential he believed he had acquired, and the "prestige" he thought was associated with being a part of management. His wife was as excited as he was and readily supported his decision to take the new job.

Jim now worked for an Acme general foreman, Teddy Smitts,

who had worked his way up after high school and twenty years in the organization. Teddy was friendly, very practical, and knew how to get things done.

Jim had been talking with Teddy over a period of time, trying to figure out what was "bugging" him—what was causing his job frustration. He asked Teddy about future potential with the company and was surprised to learn that Teddy couldn't help, since he didn't know much about Acme's future.

And it then came to Jim—he also was ignorant of Acme's future. Teddy didn't know, and he didn't know anything of the "big picture." They were both following production orders from above, and, although they followed orders well, neither was able to add anything of value to the running of the department. Jim wasn't even comfortable that he knew enough to satisfy the twenty employees working for him, who were continually asking him questions about their job security, their future potential, and the daily "whys" about their jobs.

Jim talked to his wife, and she confirmed that he had been very proud of his prior work and accomplishments as an electrician but appeared to be reticent during the last year, less assured, and certainly less happy with his job.

What's missing in Jim's job satisfaction?

Is the situation salvageable?

How can he fix the problem?

The Tools

Too often FLS's and their team don't understand how their departmental activities impact their business operationally and financially. In this Chapter, Tools are offered to assist the FLS in linking the overall financial success of the business to the success of their department.

1. Each FLS must understand the general accounting principles of "business engagement" in order to communicate effectively with their employees about the organization's business objectives.

2. Know the metrics of your organization, their history, and current challenges, and know how your competition is doing/comparing.

3. Know how your department/function is impacted by functions earlier in the process, and how you impact those later in the process.

4. Understand the basics of budgeting, why it's important, your role in the process, and how to keep track of performance (variance reporting).

5. Understand the basics of your organization's ongoing costs/expenses and where the major cost factors/opportunities for improvement reside.

6. Understand the capital expense requirements of your organization and their priorities.

7. Know the financing realities and total people costs of your organization and how those costs affect the bottom line.

8. Know how your organization makes money and who your most important and profitable customers are.

9. Know your organization's product—and what differentiates it from competitors.

10. Be familiar with the legal/regulatory process as it affects your organization.

11. Understand the basic framework of your organization's obligation to report and publicly disclose accounting/business information.

12. Understand your organization's plan for the future—and make sure this strategic plan is aligned with the performance of your employees.

13. Know your accounting organization in order to identify your resources for questions that you or your employees may have.

14. In summary, know how your organization makes and spends money (and monitors it), especially as it relates to your part of the business.

15. And understand that 90 percent of your employees will agree with 90 percent of your business decisions if you tell them, in advance, the whats and whys of your decisions.

Tips: **The FLS must know how the organization makes and spends money. If the FLS doesn't know, neither will their employees. And, in the business of your business, there are rules of the game and marketplace standards on how to "keep count." This universal language of measurement, required by many accounting and performance standards, will enable you, the FLS, to appropriately communicate the "rules" to your people.**

A Story

I first met Robert when he was just a few years from retirement. His reputation preceded him. Robert was reported to be rough and gruff. He suffered fools poorly. Robert only had a high school education. He lived on a farm forty minutes south of headquarters and sometimes his shoes (boots) were muddy when you would see him at work. He was an executive vice president of the company, and was president of the company's largest and most successful division. I worked in that division.

Robert's division had operations in four Midwest states, and he was constantly on the run, visiting all of the facilities. He always seemed to arrive unannounced, and pity the poor manager whose operation was not running in top form. It seemed everyone spent a great deal of time trying to keep track of him and decipher his travel scheme. If he had a scheme, he kept it to himself. In fact, most people tried to avoid him, to be out of the office when he arrived. This included the managers. To them it seemed that nothing good ever came from too much contact with the "big boss."

Robert seemed to know every aspect of the business. He could recite sales goals, margin targets, payroll expenses in total dollars and percent of sales, sales and marketing expenses, etc., all from memory. He knew the history of the division like his family history. Robert knew when each facility was built and why and who the first manager was. He knew the history of the first facility particularly well, since he started it and was the first manager.

One day I drew the short straw. Robert needed a driver all day, and of course no one volunteered. Everyone was too busy. As a young, first-line supervisor, I was probably the busiest person on the management team, but I was the junior member. So I took a quick break and gulped down some coffee while saying a quick rosary.

What I thought was going to be a dreadful day turned out to be one of the most formative and memorable days in my career. Robert was delightful. He knew I drew the short straw, and he was well aware of his reputation. Robert did everything he could to make me feel comfortable.

Initially Robert asked me about myself. Actually he told me about myself. Robert knew where I was from, where I went to college, my major, my interests, and my likes and dislikes. It seemed he knew that information about most of the division's "key" employees. Robert made it his business to know the management team, especially their capabilities and limitations.

I finally got up the nerve to ask Robert about his background. He asked me what I had heard and confirmed most of it while filling in some of the blanks. Robert said most people wondered how a farm boy without a college degree could become so successful in the business world. I asked him the obvious question: "Well, how did you become so successful?"

His response was simple. Robert said he always asked questions. Robert said his father told him it was too simple just to follow directions. You had to know why. Robert told me that asking questions made everything more interesting.

When he hired on the company over forty years ago as a general laborer, he just started asking questions. This trait soon set him apart from most employees. Robert knew why certain things were done a certain way. This knowledge helped him improve operations and anticipate problems.

Over the course of our day together, Robert regaled me with story after story of all of the right and wrong things he did, and what he had learned. Robert felt he needed to know every aspect of the business so that he could contribute to the company's overall success in the most effective way. And, along the way, Robert became quite successful himself.

Notes

_____

_____

_____

_____

_____

_____

_____

_____

_____

_____

_____

_____

_____

_____

_____

_____

_____

_____

_____

Notes

_____

_____

_____

_____

_____

_____

_____

_____

_____

_____

_____

_____

_____

_____

_____

_____

_____

_____

_____

_____

Chapter 3
PERFORMANCE MANAGEMENT AND COMPENSATION

The Situation

Irene was confused but determined.

Irene was recently promoted to a supervisory role over approximately twenty-five call center representatives in a 24/7 call center operation. She was one of four supervisors, and she had primary responsibility for the middle shift. There was one primary supervisor for each shift, and the fourth supervisor would fill in for the three primary shift supervisors on a rotating basis. Since the call center served a global company, the call volumes and types of calls were very similar during each shift. Each shift had a lead rep, whose main job was to take calls but had a secondary role of assisting other reps on more complicated calls. The call center reps could achieve higher pay and status through experience, training, and job knowledge.

While this particular call center was considered progressive by many standards, there was still quite a bit of employee turnover. When Irene was just starting, she enjoyed the training, fellowship, and most aspects of the job. But the one aspect of the job that confused her was the performance appraisal process. In fact, the process seemed to confuse everyone, including the supervisors and even their managers.

The process was supposed to work like this. Each new employee received a ninety-day probationary job appraisal along with a pay raise if the employee "passed." Then on each employee's anniversary date the employee was to be given a performance appraisal and, if appropriate, a merit-based pay increase (over and above any increase due to the job status ranking). The performance appraisal was two pages. The first page dealt with such measurements as basic job knowledge, attendance, ability to get along with co-workers, etc. Each measurement factor could receive a score from one to five, with one being the lowest and five being the highest. The second page was more open. It had a section for strengths and a section for weaknesses to be completed by the supervisor. The second page had another section that gave the employee an opportunity to make comments. The bottom of the second page was set for the obligatory signatures. The performance appraisal document itself seemed straightforward, and the process was set for effectiveness and efficiency. But the process was anything but effective and efficient.

The process really worked like this. With each supervisor having at least twenty-five employees, it seemed like all they were doing was preparing for the next employee performance appraisal. And the schedule was made more stressful if there were new employees receiving their ninety-day probationary appraisal. While the supervisor knew that for a number of reasons the performance appraisal process was important, she just didn't have time to execute the process correctly. So all performance appraisals were handled the same way. The supervisor sped through the process and everyone received mostly fours and a few threes and, unfortunately, everyone received the same pay adjustment.

For the employee the process seemed dysfunctional—especially to the motivated, conscientious employee. To the employee, the appraisal was received as it was given, an unavoidable, mostly thoughtless, probably legal requirement that was an annual obligation that satisfied a human resource policy that reinforced the performance management process that reached all the way to the top of the organization, *whew!* And, to the employee, everyone received the same assessment and pay adjustment. To some first-line employees, the process was demotivating and may have been a contributor to the employee turnover in the department.

And then there was the added insult that each supervisor had her own rating system. The first-shift supervisor felt her employees were superior, and she gave them all fours and a few fives, and they always received a slightly higher merit increase. Over time this approach became widely known, and all the reps wanted to work first shift, which compounded the superiority "complex."

The supervisors' boss was in a difficult position because she too was in the same type of appraisal process. In fact, this process went all the way to the CEO.

Irene thought this was just a big mess. There was no easy way an employee could identify ways to improve her performance and, worse, no way to be recognized and rewarded for the improvement. And there was no information available on how the employee's day-to-day performance impacted the company's profitability. In fact, there was little information about the company's plans or overall performance.

When Irene became a part of management she felt like she might have the opportunity to help change the business through something as basic as improving the performance appraisal process. But for a time Irene got caught up in being an overly busy supervisor and just followed everyone else. From time to time, as she was quickly completing an employee performance appraisal at midnight, she would think about how she might improve the process.

Well, one day it was announced that the CEO would be meeting with a small group of employees to listen to their ideas. Irene was selected to be a part of the first group, and she was determined to be prepared to speak her mind and make her case.

The big day arrived, and Irene was given her chance. Up to that point most employees had little to say or would only compliment the "big" boss on his deft leadership. Irene decided to speak up about the performance appraisal process, and before she knew what happened, everyone in the room had something to add about the inadequacy of the process. The "big" boss started to furiously take notes but couldn't keep up with the comments. At that point he said that it appeared the performance appraisal process needed to be reviewed and improved, if necessary, and he thought it looked necessary. On the spot he decided to form a project committee to evaluate the entire process and assigned Irene and the head of human resources to lead the project.

The "big" boss gave these basic instructions to Irene and the head of HR. He said he wanted it tied to the company's plans, consistent throughout the organization, and fair.

Is the "big" boss giving good direction?

What can be done to salvage the performance appraisal process so that it can support success?

What would you suggest?

The Tools

The role of the FLS is to administer the organization's policies and practices that have been established by senior management. Here are some of the "basics" the FLS must understand in order to knowledgably put into practice the rules of performance management.

1. The purpose of an employee performance management process (PMP) is to evaluate employees individually and as a group in order to improve their performance, thereby improving the business success of the organization.

2. The PMP is a source of continuing conversations—a reason to "sit down" with employees—and should be used for these purposes:

- compensation adjustments, paying particular attention to a "pay for performance" objective

- individual and departmental training needs assessment by identifying the organization's strengths, weaknesses, and gaps

- company succession planning to assure future management and employee skill continuation

- recognition—the "pats on the back" needed for sustained performance

- protecting your organization from lawsuits and discrimination claims

3. Evaluating employee performance is one of the most difficult if not the most difficult task an FLS has to do. (Identifying and communicating weaknesses in people you work with every day is not easy) Providing this feedback is, however, necessary and is a key responsibility of the FLS.

4. A key aspect of the PMP is the executive review of individual department performance ("scorecards"). Senior management, using available internal and external benchmarks, should evaluate each department's business performance. Some of the benchmarks will be the same company-wide, such as safety, achieving budget targets, community involvement, quality of employee communications, etc. Other benchmarks will be department specific, such as comparing advertising costs as a percentage of revenue to those of competitors' or industry standards, or comparing output per employee to historical or market data, etc.

5. We have found that a peer involvement in the PMP can bring a less emotional and more objective view of individual performance.

6. If you subscribe to a "no surprises" rule like we do, employee involvement in every step is the key. More importantly, employee involvement will likely lead to employee "buy-in," a key element in the success of the PMP. As an adjunct to this, ensure your process includes an employee self-assessment.

7. An effective PMP will also be the foundation for the company's discipline/training/growth philosophy and your (recommended) written company "official policy" on these subjects. The PMP will detect strengths and weaknesses, both individually and collectively.

8. The PMP is in the same league of importance as your company's unique business model and the planning process. Timely and clear communications, particularly by the FLS, will support the success of the PMP.

9. The PMP needs to be driven by an annual planning process. As much as practical, specific corporate goals and objectives need to be linked directly with the daily business activity all the way to the frontline employees and back to senior management.

10. The FLS needs to be directly involved in the timely and accurate business progress reports, which need to be widely communicated to all employees on a regular/scheduled basis. (Monthly? Quarterly?) In

addition, the completion of the previous year's PMP should be done as quickly and professionally as year-end results are available.

11. An individual employee's PMP needs to focus on three parts:

- an evaluation of day-to-day activities (information comes from job descriptions and skill statements)

- an evaluation of individual goals and shared departmental goals

- an evaluation of individual potential growth and development plans

12. The PMP needs to be driven by an "auditable" policy and schedule to ensure transparency and professionalism, starting with the annual business planning activity.

13. The peer review process is as important as the individual appraisal portion of the PMP. The peer review process ensures fairness and equity by supplementing an individual FLS's perceptions with the perceptions of the organization as a whole.

14. If you believe in the "pay for performance" culture as we do, then the company's total compensation plan (salary, incentives, bonuses, and benefits) must be directly linked to the PMP.

15. The "total compensation plan" must be directly related to business success and your competitiveness in the marketplace. Is the company policy to be a market compensation leader, a trailer, or somewhere in between? Will incentives, etc., be based on profitability and ability to pay, regardless of an individual's performance?

16. Employers must always assume that everyone's compensation is public knowledge. Somehow compensation details generally "leak out" to the workforce—reinforcing the need for a fair, timely, consistent, and transparent PMP and total compensation plan.

17. Fellow employees know who the "nonperformers" are—generally before you as the FLS know. Your organization's "fairness"

policies (as well as legal discrimination laws) will require a uniform and consistent treatment of these nonperformers. Discharge, generally to be avoided, may be a result after other appropriate avenues (counseling, coaching, retraining, reassignment, etc.) are exhausted. Note: violators of an organization's established, communicated policies are not included in our definition of "nonperformers."

18. FLSs must be trained on doing a PM review and how to create goals and development plans. This is not intrinsically obvious stuff.

Tips: **Good employees want to know "how they're doing" and how their performance impacts the organization. While giving honest feedback is sometimes difficult for the FLS, it's one of the keys that drive employee success. The quandary—treat everyone equally, or treat "high performers" differently? The answer *yes*! (Everyone knows the rules that apply to everyone, but the "game winners" are rewarded differently.)**

A Story

Early in my career I was completing numerous performance appraisals. I had over fifty employees and the appraisal system was driven by the employment start date so I was constantly completing and covering appraisals. The appraisal form was one sheet of paper with details on both sides. Employees were rated on a scale of one to five with five being the highest. The process lent itself to a quick but not always thoughtful review of an employee.

Well one particular time I was covering an appraisal with an employee. I was particularly busy that day so I was hustling through the process. At one point I was covering an employee's attendance rating, and I told her she got a rating of four out of five. I quickly went onto the next rating category since there would be no problem with a score of four. Before I could get into the next category she asked me if it was OK to return to the attendance category. She said she had a few questions. I said OK but asked her why she wanted to go back. She received a four out of five—pretty darn good. She asked me what it would take to get a five. She proceeded to tell me that she had never missed a day of work nor had she ever been late (in over a year) since she started. She reminded me that she always worked overtime when asked, came in early, stayed late, and came in on her day off when asked. I stopped her right there and said I had made a mistake and changed her score to a five out of five.

The moral of this story is that the performance appraisal process, regardless of the form, needs to be thoughtful and accurate. People in management and supervision can't forget how important the appraisal process is to all employees. The good ones won't let you get away with sloppy work, and everyone will be looking for fundamental fairness—accuracy, consistency, and uniformity in application.

By the way, I married that employee several years later, and we have been married for over thirty-three years as of this writing.

Notes

_____

_____

_____

_____

_____

_____

_____

_____

_____

_____

_____

_____

_____

_____

_____

_____

_____

_____

_____

_____

Chapter 4:

COMMUNICATIONS AND EMPLOYEE RELATIONS

The Situation

Maggie saw herself as a very effective supervisor. She was responsible for the daily management of twenty-four dispatchers. The dispatchers worked in six (four per location) separate geographic locations and were responsible for scheduling and coordinating the work of anywhere from one hundred individuals and crews on a very slow day to over two hundred on a very busy day. It seemed as though more contract crews were added to their dispatch list on a weekly basis. Most of the work was scheduled on paper at that time, but computer-aided dispatching was being tested in another location.

The computer-aided technology would allow the "work" to flow directly from the "work request" to the individual service truck or crew vehicle. This meant the service specialists and crew trucks could move directly to the work without coming to the office to receive the work instructions and the day's schedule. This technology could save hundreds of hours of "administrative" time. In theory the work could begin nearly immediately every morning—if the technology and software worked. And, at last report, the technology and software were working in the test mode, and the union-represented employees were actually warming up to using the new technology in the truck.

Maggie had a great background for her job. She had been a service specialist for several years in a smaller location and then moved into the dispatcher position. That was a bit of a difficult decision for her because she had to leave the union, but she felt good about her background and wanted a new challenge.

In a small location a service specialist would have to deal with all sorts of work. In the larger work locations, service specialists would only do certain types of work while others would do the other, more physical type of work. The union contract didn't protect certain types of work, but in the larger locations the union members were very particular about the type of work they would do. Because Maggie had worked in a small location and was required, like her colleagues, to do everything, when she became a supervisor over a number of field dispatchers she had no patience for the employees of the larger work locations who wanted to pick and choose their work.

While Maggie was working as a service specialist, the company went through a significant field reorganization. The reorganization did result in job reductions, but the impact on the workforce was not significant. The company offered an early retirement program, and nearly everyone who wanted to stay had a job, and many had the chance for a promotion. Maggie got a promotion.

Maggie liked the way things were going with the company. Like everyone she wasn't pleased with everything, but she liked the improved communications employed by top management. Management even came around on an annual basis, and there were quarterly business meetings scheduled to review the company financials and other universal topics. She felt like she was working for a progressive company. A 401k program was introduced, and after a few years a bonus plan was put in place for all employees. Individual "freestanding" department communication "silos" were being replaced with company-wide dialogue.

Then one summer the natural flow of the company seemed to be interrupted. Everyone in the company knew the annual budget and business plan was presented to the Board of Directors at the July board meeting. Over the past four to five years it seemed everyone pitched in to help develop this annual budget and business plan, and this year was no different. Everything was on schedule except the post-board meeting communication. You could set not just your calendar but your watch on it—but not this year. A few days grew into a few weeks that grew into a month. Everyone was beginning to wonder. Top management gave some positive comments, but no one was reassured.

It turned out that the board was dissatisfied with management's growth projections. The board felt management was being too conservative and too comfortable. The board gave management a growth target that seemed unattainable to management at the time. The management team needed time to process the entire situation. They didn't know if it was achievable. While management was working day and night to develop a new business plan, they failed to communicate to employees. Management had forgotten how interested and involved the employees were in the success of the business. A real employee "meltdown" was in the making. Clearly without the support of all the employees the new plan would be difficult to execute.

Maggie and many other supervisors felt the confusion. While worrying about the worst possible outcome of any new plan, she still wanted to help. At the next quarterly meeting, Maggie spoke up to management. She asked the CFO what was going on and how she and her fellow employees could help. Maggie said in her opinion productivity had decreased while employees were discussing rumors involving a major down-sizing to a possible sale of the business. After brief reflection, the CFO told Maggie a team of senior managers were being assigned to the project and that the project would include employee involvement at all levels. It would also include improved communications.

Given the work environment over the past five years and considering the CFO's comments would you as a supervisor be reassured at the present time?

What do you think management could have done differently after the board meeting? Was timing a consideration?

As the FLS, how do you feel as the main communication conduit, the "credible messenger," to your the employees in your organization?

What message would you take back to your employees now?

What advice would you give to management going forward?

Do you feel good about your company? Were you surprised?

The Tools

We have found that the FLS is frequently a "credible messenger" from employer to employees in any organization, but too often doesn't have all the skills or communications experience to be effective. In this Chapter, Tools and Tips are provided to aid the FLS in becoming an effective communicator.

1. We have included employee communications in this book because in our experience it's the capstone, of critical importance, the archway of employee morale and ultimately business success, especially with younger generations of employees, who have differing expectations of employment.

2. As employers you can do everything right with respect to compensation, benefits, uniform policies, etc., and, yet, without effective communications you will not achieve your business goals.

3. To us communications is always open, two way, involving great attention to "listening," is generally of an oral nature and has the objective of developing and maintaining boss/employee relationships and an environment (developed culture) of openness and credibility.

4. All employees are a vital part of the organization. There is no "us and them." Everyone needs to know the business details of what drives their own job success and what makes the organization run. Of course there are certain issues that need to be confidential—acquisitions, mergers, unusual changes in top management, etc. But on a day-to-day operating basis, all employees need to know all of the information needed to help the company be successful.

5. Company leadership is responsible for establishing the culture and needs to set the tone, identify the communications methodology (internal communications process—ICP), and define the message on an annual, quarterly, monthly, weekly, and daily basis. The ICP is the work product of leadership and cannot be driven from the bottom up. Leadership must understand that the role of effective

communications within an organization cannot be delegated—it must come from the top.

6. The main objective of the ICP is to connect the company mission, vision, objectives, etc., to every individual in the company. Each employee should be able to articulate, correctly, in their own words, the company mission, vision, objectives, etc., and the role they play in their job in achieving success.

7. The direct supervisor/frontline supervisor has a principal role in the ICP. They are the credible messengers. If they don't understand the message, then their employees most likely won't understand. The FLS/DS needs to understand the company's business model and be able to clearly articulate it to their employees.

8. Always err on the side of too much communication. Written forms of communication such as employee handbooks, newsletters, letters to home, etc., should always reinforce the verbal messages. These written forms of communication are wonderful ways to ensure consistency and uniformity of message.

9. Our experience tells us that one breakdown in the communication link (ICP) will be a potential problem or a missed opportunity for the organization. Most union organizing drives and most grievances/complaints result from a communication breakdown in the immediate relationship between employee and supervisor.

10. Company leadership needs to ensure there is a balance to all aspects of the enterprise. Employees today want to be proud working for a company that is successful but also shares that success not only with employees but with the community. In our experience, companies that encourage and support their employees in community involvement have a more productive workforce.

11. The American workforce today is skeptical of Wall Street and most of corporate America. Employees want to be proud of their employer and work for a successful company. Leadership must define success and articulate the definition throughout the organization. Everyone must be clear on the organization's way of

doing business. And, the talk must clearly and consistently be walked. Your employees are looking for more than mere compliance.

12. The company should also define and internally publish a "fairness" doctrine. This doctrine, an adjunct or addendum to the organization's ethics policy, would include guidelines for compensation, recognition, promotions, job assignments, job security, and discipline.

13. The company needs to operate under the "no surprises" rule. This means first and foremost that employees should never be surprised by the results of a performance appraisal, compensation adjustment, or application of reward or discipline. The "no surprises" rule should apply to changes in all company policy, business direction, and any significant changes in compensation and benefits. Many companies announce these types of changes in e-mail "scud missiles." This type of communication style always results in reduced employee morale and productivity. If possible, employees need to be focused on their jobs and not worrying about unknown or unexpected changes in compensation, company benefits, or the business environment.

14. Peer employee involvement should be encouraged and built into the ICP. Peer interaction supports an increase in an organization's joint knowledge and advances company teamwork and overall communication.

15. It is important that each employee feels they have a voice and, more importantly, that they actually do have a voice, in the success of the company. Every employee needs to believe that the company embraces the concept of fundamental fairness, and everyone in the organization needs to "walk the talk." Work rules and policies are for everyone.

16. Don't forget, the communication process should include business results, business forecasts, business issues, and what is going on in the company. Remember, everyone wants to work for a successful company. Define success, communicate its definition, measure it, reward it, and *communicate your success!*

Tips: As an FLS, you can "correctly" abide by the organization's policies and procedures, and yet fail in effective employee communications and involvement. Ever heard of the story where one specific message is passed individually down a line of people? The message received by the last individual generally bears no resemblance to the original message.

A Story

At one point in my career I was working in management for a privately owned regional retailer that eventually became part of a highly successful national chain.

During one of my senior-level management courses we were studying the importance of the alignment of a company's mission, vision, values/culture, goals and objectives, and policies and procedures (a company's value and performance model) to ensure business success. The belief was that it would be difficult for a company to achieve optimum business success if there were inconsistencies in the alignment and communication of the value and performance model. As a project for the course, I set out to do a study of my company's value and performance model.

The first thing I did after clearing my project plan with the course professor was to go to my immediate boss. He thought it was a great idea. The first step in my project plan was to interview all of the senior officers of the company. Since there was no published value and performance model, I was hoping to get the information from the senior team. As part of the interview process I was hoping to learn the linkage of the various division and department goals and objectives. Well, to my great surprise I was told by each senior officer that either a value and performance model existed, but it was none of the employees' business, or even that beyond the secret division budgets there was no value and performance model for the company. A year or so later the company was sold to another business for a fraction of the original value.

The moral here is that possessing a solid value and performance model may not always guarantee business success, but not communicating the model to employees will certainly make the task of achieving success more difficult.

Notes

Notes

Chapter 5

LEGAL REQUIREMENTS

The Situation

As a new supervisor, Jim was intent on avoiding the many employment-related legal pitfalls he had been told about. Time and again, his boss had drilled into him the "don't do this, don't do that" lectures, that "no discrimination" was the rule, and that, above all, Jim was to always treat his employees equally.

Jim thought that equal treatment was easy enough to say and to require but difficult to understand because his employees were not all equal. Some were smarter, some were faster, and some were more conscientious about attendance and doing a good job. But Jim knew that the "law was the law," a part of the business of supervising employees, and that he had to do his best to comply.

He memorized the "no no's "of discrimination—no discrimination in gender, age, nationality, color, race, religion, or physical/mental disabilities.

After awhile, it became awkward and uncomfortable for Jim to treat all his employees the same. He found himself trying to assign the good jobs equally among his employees, regardless of their abilities. He found himself recommending the same levels of merit increases, even though Jim knew that a number of his employees were much stronger productive workers. He was even avoiding talking to several of his employees who were having problems at home, because he was afraid that the time spent with them might be perceived as favoritism.

Jim was not happy as a supervisor. He wondered if he was being overly sensitive to the discrimination rules that had been drilled into him. He knew that even his employees wondered about many of his actions and decisions.

What was Jim missing in his education about equal opportunity?

Is it all about "no-no's"—what not to do?

Can Jim actually treat his employees unequally?

The Tools

Frequently, when faced with difficult or complicated employee situations, the FLS will rely on instinct or intuition to solve the problem. This "what seems right" approach may lead to legal problems for the FLS and their organization. Using the following Tools and utilizing available legal resources will help avoid these problems.

1. The FLS must understand at least the basics of the American legal system—the workings of executive, legislative, and judicial branches of the government, and the roles they play in your business.

2. Employees should all know the ethical policies and commitments of your organization and their role in assuring compliance. They must understand the concept that legal compliance is part of running a business and is their responsibility.

3. The FLS must know when to alert the experts when they might encounter certain issues (such as discrimination allegations) that may have an impact beyond their own department.

4. The FLS (as well as all management) must have a general understanding of employment and labor law and how these laws impact your employees and your organization. Your employees, depending on the size of the organization, may well be protected against discrimination in hiring, firing, compensation and benefits, etc., by a number of federal and local laws—for example, laws preventing:

- Retaliation against complaining employees

- Unsafe or unhealthy work conditions and practices, as provided by the Occupational Safety and Health Act

- Discrimination (treating people differently) *because of* race, gender, nationality, religion, age over forty, disability, or veteran status, under various civil rights legislation; sexual harassment prevention is a critical ingredient

- Discrimination against union representatives and union organizing under the National Labor Relations Act (which also prohibits certain unfair labor practices in dealing with your employees, even if they aren't unionized)

- Overtime without proper pay, under the Fair Labor Standards Act (which also requires certain minimum wages)

- Various employer disciplinary actions against personnel protected by the Family and Medical Leave Act (because of personal or family health issues, adoptions, etc.)

5. FLSs should be aware of sensitive issues within the organization and their individual department (history, concerns, and activity).

6. The FLS must be sure to document any legal issues for possible future reference (and be trained to use existing organization forms that are used in the regular course of business).

7. All employees should be encouraged to discuss employment problems and any potential legal issues with their FLS, in order to promote an internal resolution process that provides uniform and consistent remedies throughout the organization. Helpful in this process is an FLS awareness of "conflict management" principles, mediation approaches, and using the HR or personnel function as an "intervener." The organization's culture should promote escalating unresolved issues to the next level of supervision. (Don't let issues "die" at the first step.)

Tips: **"Part and parcel" of running any company or organization is legal compliance, particularly compliance with laws protecting employees. Most organizations at one time or another have been exposed to the potential of an employee lawsuit, and employees today are more aware of "legal rights." The FLS is literally the "front line" of avoiding these legal issues and their potentially significant monetary liabilities.**

The FLS must understand the organization's culture and ethical policies/commitments to employees (and to customers, suppliers and the community at large).

A Story

I was confronted by an aggressive employee who was claiming that his religious freedoms were being abridged. He didn't assert any Title VII claims but did insist that he be allowed to pray during his lunchtime. And he had one other demand—he must be allowed to pray at the highest point in the building, which happened to be the steel roofing superstructure over the factory floor. He had actually climbed up a ladder onto a steel beam, spreading his prayer rug across a ten-inch-wide beam, thirty feet above the floor. The employer presented several alternatives, but he insisted on his "rights" and continued his daily climb, claiming that he was on his own time and his employer shouldn't interfere with his exercise of his religious freedoms. He was warned to stop and was progressively disciplined, ending with a suspension and ultimate employment discharge. The employee hired a lawyer, a discrimination charge was filed, and the EEOC ultimately found "no probable cause" to believe discrimination was involved. The agency agreed that we had reasonably attempted to accommodate the employee's religious beliefs and that our refusal to allow superstructure climbing was within our rights. The employee's safety under OSHA, and our liability under workers' compensation, precluded any superstructure climbing.

Notes

Notes

Chapter 6

RECRUITING, HIRING, AND RETENTION

The Situation

Herb was really frustrated this week. He had an employee call in sick and another employee had quit. Herb was up against it once again. He had clients that were scheduled for service that night, and he was now two employees short. He needed help.

Herb supervises a group of ten people who provide in-home, nonmedical health care services such as light housekeeping, cooking and food preparation, assisting with laundry, shopping, etc. A total of six supervisors oversee the schedules and duties of about sixty home service representatives. These jobs don't require any sort of technical degree or certification. Herb's company provides services on a 24/7 basis and generally each company representative works with the same clients. From time to time someone else from the supervisor's group will serve a different client in order to cover for vacations and personal days. These schedule modifications can be managed easily with enough advance notification. When people call in sick, don't show up for work, or simply quit, the scheduling becomes quite challenging. When these unscheduled absences occur, a service representative from another group may be called in on a day off to cover the clients. This often results in un-needed overtime. And, frequently the service level to the client declines because of the unfamiliarity of the employee to the specific customer needs.

Most of the client fees are paid for by Medicare/Medicaid or private insurance. The payment process is rather straightforward and Herb's company receives a steady cash flow. But the payment provider in many cases certifies the service provider and monitors and audits the provider's customer service levels. If Herb's company does not provide adequate client service, they can lose their contract. The supervisors are aware of this fact of business life, and they also know they must control expenses. As usual, the frontline supervisor is "on the front line" where the "battle is either lost or won."

Each supervisor is awarded a monthly bonus if they hit their financial goals and their customer service goals. Each goal is measured separately, and the supervisor can receive bonus money for one without receiving bonus money for the other measure. There is more bonus value placed on the financial goals than on the customer service goals. Consequently, on a monthly basis customer service is sacrificed for financial goals.

To the supervisor, it seems there is never enough time to properly train the frontline employee because the supervisor must get the employee in front of the client as soon as possible. Consequently, the new employee is generally unprepared, and the client is frustrated by the poor level of service. Employees may grow frustrated and either call in sick or abruptly quit—leaving the supervisor to cover the client calls with another employee on overtime. And, the client may report poor service, which brings pressure on management to improve, resulting in pressure rolling downhill to the supervisor.

Every supervisor struggles with these same problems. They would complain to each other on a regular basis, but they never felt empowered to tackle the problem themselves, and they never had the time to explain their concerns to their boss. The group did meet once a month on an informal basis for beer and pizza, and Herb decided he would surface the problems once again to his peers. He was determined to get his colleagues to focus on the problem and develop some ideas to improve results.

After the first couple of beers Herb brought up the problems of absenteeism, scheduling, cost management, and poor service levels. Initially the supervisors were all over the place with thoughts and ideas, but Herb was able to focus the group somewhat on potential solutions. Each supervisor, however, was afraid to become too creative for fear of jeopardizing their bonus plan.

The supervisors agreed that there were solid, well-trained employees who took their work seriously. And this group of employees shared some common characteristics—dependability, knowing their clients well, and always doing their work with a professional flair. This group was always called upon to pull the overtime and do the extra work to help the company. But there simply weren't enough of them. The challenge, then, was to find more new employees that shared the same characteristics as these employees. The initial question was how to get started. Herb agreed to approach their new boss, Alice, for her advice and help.

The supervisors' new boss was, in fact, very new to the organization. Alice had been recently hired away from a major competitor, and her reputation preceded her. She was known to be tough and demanding but open to ideas—especially those that led to improvements. Herb approached her with some uncertainty.

Herb found Alice to be open and engaging but all business. Alice wanted to know what was on Herb's mind. Herb was well prepared and described the business issues and challenges clearly. Alice listened intently, asking a few clarifying questions along the way. When Herb finished, Alice smiled. Alice told Herb that he had described a challenging but not unusual set of work problems related to this area. Alice told Herb that the newer frontline employees appeared to be poorly trained and poorly prepared for their client work. This was caused by the organization's focus on monthly financial results—get the service reps out in front of the client as quickly as possible in order to minimize overtime and to serve more clients. Consequently, financials were hurt by the unnecessary overtime, and service levels to clients were impacted negatively by the poorly trained employees.

Alice suggested to Herb that she attend the next informal supervisors' meeting, and she would buy the beer and pizza if they agreed to put their heads together to commit to sensible solutions. Alice hinted to Herb that she believed the solutions started initially with more attention to hiring and then consistent focus on training. Alice said to Herb, "The ultimate solution to these problems is tied to the things we do well at the beginning of the process. And, come prepared to discuss your current compensation plan in a constructive way."

Was Alice on track with her comments on hiring and training?

What about training in this situation? Is it that important? What about orientation to the industry, business, company, and client? Does anyone really know what that is or what that means?

How can the hiring process be developed to more accurately hire the right individuals?

Are all of the costs of running this very important part of the business really understood by anyone in the organization?

Is there a link between the type of client served and the type of person employed? Think diversity.

The Tools

All management, particularly the FLS, needs to be periodically involved in the employment process, and therefore *must*:

1. Understand the total costs (direct pay, benefits, and taxes) of an employee, and the cumulative cost burden on the organization.

2. Determine the core competencies the organization needs for each position—the actual skill/knowledge/experience requirements (not preferences) of any required position. Use a current job description that uses a standardized format across the organization.

3. Be able to assess alternatives to a needed regular employee (part time, contracted, borrowed, temporary, etc.).

4. Be skilled in assessing the real need for any additional employees. Are there options (combining jobs, overtime, eliminating unnecessary work, technology, etc.)?

5. Review likely sources of candidates, with due consideration to diversity objectives. (You should always be on the lookout for *all* talent and talent resources.)

6. Know how to save time by preliminarily screening candidates (by phone, screening resumes, etc.), using the same written criteria and documentation for all "screeners."

7. Schedule face to face "team" interviews, involving others that will also rely on the new hire. Interviewers must be knowledgeable on selection processes (for example, using "behavior interviewing" techniques that focus on actual past behaviors in certain situations) for identifying the "best" candidates and how to "market" the organization well while being clear about the organization's expectations.

8. Do reference/education/criminal checks, and test if appropriate (including drug screens), and once satisfied, offer the position conditioned on the results (founded on equitable and uniformly applied compensation policy).

9. Orient the new hire extensively and assure frequent performance reviews during the "probationary" period. This is particularly important for entry-level new hires—those without much prior work experience.

10. Decide on an acceptable level of employee "turnover", recognizing the significant expense in hiring and training replacements for those that leave. Minimizing turnover is a function of:

- Hiring "right" in the first place (assuring new hire core competencies)

- Leadership's philosophy of communications, the PMP, etc.

- The FLS assuring proper communications, feedback, involvement, and job challenges/business understanding of employees

- Investing in employees through training and development efforts

- The organization's assurance that the total compensation program (salaries, benefits, and incentives) are competitive in the marketplace, and that employees understand this. (Plans need not be "equal" to the marketplace.)

Tips: **Employees in many organizations constitute the majority of annual operating expenses. Once you know their average cost, you may well hesitate to hire a new one. (Especially if you consider how easy it is to hire someone now, and how difficult it is to "fire" someone in the future.)**

But once the decision to "add to the payroll" is made, the best possible candidate for any level job must be selected. No unqualified friends, relatives, or needed "warm bodies" should be considered.

Bad hires are expensive, but good hires drive your organization's success.

A Story

Years ago I worked for a large regional retail operation. One of the stores was located in a major university town, and business always increased dramatically once the college kids came back into town. Our store always needed to build its workforce as the kids came back. Most of the new employees were hired as cashiers. I had recommended to the daughter of a close friend of mine that she apply for a job at that store as a cashier. I assured my friend that they always needed help, especially as the college kids returned.

My friend's daughter applied for a job and was hired "on the spot." She was to start the next day for her orientation and training. She was very excited, and my friend thought incorrectly that I had pulled some strings. I called the store the next day and told the store manager about my friend's daughter. The store manager said he not only knew the story but had already met my friend's daughter. I was feeling pretty good about my recommendation to my friend to have his daughter apply for a job at this store. Golly, she had been there one day, and the boss had already met her. At this point the store manager asked me if I wanted to talk with her and immediately transferred my call to an extension phone somewhere in the store.

As my friend's daughter picked up the phone I could hear all of this noise. I asked her how she was doing, and she said fine under the circumstances. I asked her, "What circumstances?" She told me that she was running a cash register and had been on that register for over four hours without a break, on her first day, with only a few hours training. This was before the days of bar codes and computerized registers with most of the merchandise coming to the register without price tickets. I asked her how she was coping, and she told me that she would get on the PA and ask for assistance, and if that didn't come soon enough, she would ask the cashier next to her if she knew the price. The cashier always knew the price, unless the customer knew it better. The cashier next to my friend's daughter was an old-timer at the store—she had been there a week. A regular employee told her the key to running a quick cash register was linked to the ability to make up prices that were acceptable to the customer.

Unfortunately, this type of management culture with respect to hiring and training was too prevalent throughout the company. The company was sold in twelve months. Within one year of the new owners gaining control, only four of the 160 store management employees under the previous owners remained employed.

Notes

Notes

_____

_____

_____

_____

_____

_____

_____

_____

_____

_____

_____

_____

_____

_____

_____

_____

_____

Chapter 7

TRAINING AND DEVELOPMENT

The Situation

Debra had worked in her company's accounting department for almost six years.

Although she had no formal accounting education, she had worked in accounting for a prior employer and now had over ten years of total accounting/clerical experience. She was a quick learner and was feeling comfortable about her accounts payable and accounts receivable processing responsibilities. She got along very well with the other ten people in her section and enjoyed the respect she received when fellow employees would seek out her advice on work-related problems.

And then her world changed. Her boss, section supervisor Myra Goodfellow, quit because of her spouse's job relocation, and Debra was offered the supervisor's job vacated by Myra. The chief of accounting didn't give Debra much time to think about the opportunity, assuring her that she was perfect for the job. After all, Debra knew the payables and receivables systems, knew and enjoyed working with all her fellow employees, and was a "natural" fit to replace Myra.

Debra liked the extra money offered to her, and although she had never supervised other people, readily accepted the promotion.

For the first few weeks, the new job went smoothly for Debra. She basically continued providing advice for her direct reports and didn't see much change from her old position. Gradually, however, she saw that different new demands were being made on her by upper-level accounting management, including requests for productivity assessments and reports on department improvements, requests for updates on employee performance for the merit budget, and directions to improve the absenteeism rates in her section.

Debra had no experience in dealing with any of these issues and didn't know where to begin. She talked to her own boss, who obviously was busy with other issues, and was told to check with the personnel department for help.

The personnel department did provide Debra with a number of forms for use in evaluating her employees and for monitoring absenteeism. They couldn't help her with the department business issues, telling her that she "would know a lot more about those issues than the personnel department."

Debra was now becoming concerned about her own job performance. She herself had been through a number of performance evaluations in the past but was uncomfortable about sitting down with her "friends" to discuss their performance and possible shortcomings. She also hesitated to get involved with any discussions about absenteeism, since she knew that a number of her friends did have high absence rates, clearly unjustified because of personal issues that Debra didn't want to confront. And the business reports and demands being made on her by management were not clear to her, and she didn't know how to solve the problems.

Debra was starting to lose sleep. She wondered whether she had done the right thing in accepting the promotion. Maybe it was time to move on.

Was Debra the perfect candidate for Myra's job?

What, if anything, could Debra's company have done to reduce her frustration?

What could Debra have done differently?

The Tools

In our experience, meaningful training and development opportunities for all employees are as much a motivator as salaries and benefits. Successful organizations have a reputation for developing their employees, and the marketplace is generally aware of their commitment to training. This commitment will always be a valuable tool in any recruiting efforts. We believe if you use the tools in this chapter, your organization will have an advantage when recruiting new employees and retaining existing employees.

1. Employees are a valuable asset. Appropriate training and development of your people will increase their asset value. Training shows that you do care about them and want to increase their value.

2. Employees view their own training as a huge positive. The training is seen as meaningful to their own long-term career plans and, ultimately, their own job security in the marketplace.

3. Training may well be your #1 motivator for employees, going beyond any other salary or benefit considerations. Resulting improved employee attitude and morale will also improve their productivity.

4. A commitment to vigorous training and development programs will make your organization more attractive to potential employees and, when properly focused, will keep your employees and company more competitive.

5. The individual employee has a very important role to play in identifying his or her own personal and professional career and training needs. In fact, discussing future training and development needs and opportunities with employees is one way to help the employer identify their high-potential candidates.

6. Many small to medium-sized companies don't have the staff to manage all the steps of the training function—from needs identification to the application and execution of training programs.

So, how do you start? A well designed performance management process (PMP) will help employers identify core individual, departmental, and company-wide training needs. Stick to your core, and, although many needs can be met internally, it sometimes may be necessary to reach outside for expert help.

7. Make sure your PMP process includes a gap analysis that identifies the gaps between the skills/abilities that employees *need* to perform well versus what they currently demonstrate. These gaps need to be quickly addressed.

8. A skill gap analysis for those "promotable" (the "successors" to current job holders) needs also to be performed to ensure developmental plans for future leadership.

9. Resulting training plans are to be focused on the core needs identified in a gap analysis (per the PMP).

10. There should be training resources devoted to general "core" topics such as safety, customer service/satisfaction, diversity, quality, and continuous improvement, as well as basic accounting, finance, and operating results.

11. The company should have a formal policy focused on external training and development such as programs for college degrees and technical/professional certifications such as a CPA.

12. Regardless of size, a company needs to know its future employee needs. This is the point where the formal planning process intersects with the marketing plan and the company training plan. How you manage your business growth with your employee growth (both skills and numbers of employees) will determine to a large degree how successful you will be in the future. This works for downsizing as well.

13. Ensure that any training mandated by Law (e.g., safety training) is received in a timely manner. Documentation of such should also be completed to evidence compliance.

14. Training effectiveness should be formally evaluated (i.e., has

performance or behavior actually changed, as planned?). Offerings should be modified based on the results of the evaluation.

Tips: Training is an investment in the future, not an expense to be avoided. It will advance the knowledge base of your employees and ultimately improve your organization's productivity and quality. Employees value the attention and investment in them, and the best possible job candidates will be attracted by your training reputation.

A Story

A relatively new "metric" has recently appeared on many business measurement agendas—the metric of training hours per employee.

Successful organizations generally attribute their overall success to a limited number of factors. Maybe it's the uniqueness of their product or product design. Maybe it's the pricing of their product—their ability to produce more efficiently than their competitors. Maybe it's the quality of their product or the quality of their processes that enable higher efficiencies. Or maybe it's their people that make the difference. If it's a people factor, these organizations generally will take great pride in the amount of training they are investing in employees. And they'll explain it as such—maximizing a return on their investment in employees.

Training hours per employee can be a high number—some organizations advertise up to two hundred hours per year, which is five full-time weeks of training, on average, for each employee. Not all employees get the same amount; some may get higher or lower, and the employers are careful to explain that their investments are not "training for the sake of training" but are carefully thought out, based on their own assessments of "needs."

Needs are different for each organization and industry. Fast-moving technology companies need constant updating of employee skills in order to keep up with or exceed the state of industry technology. Companies with low margins in mature markets may invest in employee skill development in order to survive, by combining jobs and improving productivity/pricing.

ROI on training is problematic. We've learned over the years that the returns are clearly there (if they're based on real needs)—but difficult or impossible to measure.

Notes

Notes

_____

_____

_____

_____

_____

_____

_____

_____

_____

_____

_____

_____

_____

_____

_____

_____

_____

_____

_____

Chapter 8
LABOR AND UNION RELATIONS

The Situation

Jim was a bit uncomfortable. He'd been newly appointed from an hourly paid nonexempt job to his supervisory position about a year ago, and so far he'd been able to keep up with the hectic pace of work while getting along with most of his employees. He was a bit disappointed, however, that the promised training for him never came about, and now the scuttlebutt was that his employer would be cutting back and reducing the workforce.

Jim decided that the best thing for him to do was to stay below the radar screen and keep his nose clean. He needed this job.

And to top it off, Jim was noticing some unusual things around the office. Employees who he thought were his friends appeared to be avoiding him. It also seemed like whenever Jim ran into a group of employees, they'd suddenly stop talking until Jim had passed by. He'd also noticed groups of employees in the parking lot after work, congregating around someone who Jim didn't recognize. Jim didn't want to seem paranoid, so he didn't mention these occurrences to anyone.

And then Jim had a series of confrontations with several of his employees. They had "grouped up" and together asked Jim about the reduction in force rumors they were hearing. Jim didn't have any answers and, when asked, couldn't tell them how a reduction in force would be managed. By seniority? By department? How would management reductions differ from hourly employee reductions? Jim didn't know and so advised his employees.

One of Jim's favorite employees finally asked to meet with him in private. She told Jim that because of job security concerns and supervision's general inability to answer any of their questions, many of her fellow employees were thinking of joining a union. Jim was surprised—and scared. He knew that a union was the last thing his employer wanted, especially in these economically difficult times.

Although Jim didn't exactly know how to handle the situation, he at least knew that he'd better try—and try without any help. He was not about to surface this issue to upper management since he'd seen too many "messengers of bad news" suffer in the past.

Jim told his employee that she needed to pass the word. This was a serious issue. Unionization could well be calamitous to his employer, and people needed to know that they could all lose their jobs if the company went out of business. Rank and file union promoters, at least, could lose their job if they continued insisting on a union. Jim also asked her to keep an eye out, and let him know of any new news or events. If possible, she was even to attend any union meetings and let Jim know what was happening. She agreed to act on his behalf.

Jim was upset, and decided to meet with several of the employees who had previously confronted him. He told them that he'd heard of a possible union organizing attempt and wanted them to know that he thought they were "nuts." Jim told them he'd been in a union at a prior employer and "was sick of paying the union dues, of being on strike with no pay, and of not having any say in the business." He also told them that his understanding was that union representation in the country was going down, not up, and that maybe only 12 percent of American workers were in a union, compared to the 35 percent of union members in the 1950s, when his dad was a kid. He warned them about the serious consequences of unionization.

Did Jim take the right approach?

What else could/should he have done?

Are there any legal ramifications to Jim's approach?

Why do employees join unions?

Why don't employers generally support the establishment of unions?

The Tools

All management and particularly the FLSs with hourly paid or "nonexempt "employees should generally be exposed to a short course of study to:

1. Review the history of employee "concerted efforts," collective bargaining, and unionization in America to understand the principles and issues involved.

2. Review the highlights of the National Labor Relations Act and its amendments and rules to understand the foundations of current American labor law in the private sector. Review, if appropriate, other federal and state laws applying to the public sector (government jobs).

3. Understand the critical role of the FLS in union avoidance and organizing, collective bargaining, and contract administration. Note that the majority of union organizing efforts may result directly from communications and relationship issues with immediate supervisors.

4. Know the whys and why nots of union representation. Unions are generally expensive, but once you have one, understand that their objectives include your business success—they are a "stakeholder," and you need to "partner" with them to avoid an adversary relationship ("us versus them").

5. Understand the critical importance of regular, credible, two-way communications with your employees.

6. FLSs with union-represented employees must be trained to understand their collective bargaining agreement (CBA) and how to avoid/resolve grievances.

7. Understand concepts of fundamental fairness (consistency and uniformity of employee treatment, etc.) and what employees expect of management and the FLS.

Most employers in the United States are adverse to union representation of their employees, primarily because of the threat of strikes, the usual increased administrative costs, and the possible loss of productivity. Union "avoidance," therefore, becomes a necessary part of running their business, and care must be taken to avoid the many legal pitfalls enumerated under National Labor Relations Act rulings. Unfair labor practices (ULPs), for example, prohibit employers (and their agent supervisors) from threatening, interrogating, making promises to, or spying on union reps or their supporters (who have effectively become a special "protected class" of employees).

Tips: **Because of the recent reduction in union representation rates in the United States, unionization may be on a comeback in America, and the FLSs must know their** *critical* **role in either avoiding a unionization of employees or, more effectively, administering a negotiated collective bargaining agreement. Treat employees consistently and uniformly (e.g., in communications, community involvement, etc.) regardless of union affiliation.**

A Story

The two authors have each (separately and together) been directly involved in the three major aspects of unionization in America: union organizing, union contract (CBA—collective bargaining agreement) negotiations , and CBA administration.

Both authors, given their druthers, would avoid employee union representation if possible, for two major reasons: the possibility of a strike (even though perfectly legal) can cripple or destroy any organization, and the almost certain additional costs that arise in administering union-represented employees in the day-to-day activities of a business. Most of the historic reasons for unionization in this country have been dealt with by the enactment of multiple and various federal and state laws designed to protect the American worker. Health and safety, antidiscrimination, overtime payments, minimum wage, child labor laws, family leaves, etc., are all laws designed to protect workers from abuses suffered in the past, which in turn led to union efforts to protect their members. A strong argument can be made that unions are no longer necessary as long as employees are treated uniformly and with consistency, with respect and dignity, by their employer and FLS.

On the other hand, businesses can certainly be run efficiently and competitively with a union-represented workforce. Unions effectively force employers to treat employees objectively and with fairness. CBAs can certainly be negotiated to be wage and benefit cost competitive, to recognize skill and experience over seniority, and to provide for efficient work rules and practices. What it takes is mutual trust and respect, with an ongoing relationship committed to maximize employee and employer interests.

Ultimately, most unions recognize that successful employers are in the union's best interest—especially for purposes of long-term employee job security.

One of the authors, by the way, was a union-represented employee doing summer manufacturing work during college. The author was fired, inappropriately, in violation of the collective bargaining agreement, for taking time off to attend a family member's funeral. Only through the intercession of the union was the author reinstated and ultimately able to afford completion of undergraduate school.

Notes

_____

_____

_____

_____

_____

_____

_____

_____

_____

_____

_____

_____

_____

_____

_____

_____

_____

_____

_____

Notes

_____

_____

_____

_____

_____

_____

_____

_____

_____

_____

_____

_____

_____

_____

_____

_____

_____

_____

_____

Chapter 9

LEADERSHIP AND TEAM BUILDING

The Situation

Bill was as encouraged by business as he had ever been. His store was finally becoming profitable. Bill ran a department store that had never been profitable in its five-year existence. He had been transferred there just a few months ago, and his boss told him that if the store was not profitable in a year it would be closed. It was the worst performing store in the company.

Before Bill took the job as the store manager, he went for a quiet visit. Since no one knew him, Bill was able to walk the store freely. The store was a mess in every way. But Bill saw the potential for success. He knew it would be a big challenge, but he took the job anyway. Interestingly, the CEO seemed to take great interest in the store and met with Bill several times before he started his new assignment. The CEO was ever present in the company's forty-five stores, as was his entire senior management team. More importantly, they always wanted to help in any way they could.

The CEO had been with the company about two years. Once he arrived and assembled his management team, the company started to grow again, and, more importantly, profits grew as well. The CEO's style of managing by walking around had everyone excited and on their toes. You never knew when the "old man" would show up at your store. You always wanted to be at your best.

Bill was as excited as everyone else in the company. Bill and his new team cleaned up the store and filled it with merchandise. Both sales and profits started to grow. It seemed every employee in the store was excited with the exception of one, Big John, the receiving department manager.

Big John had retired five years ago as the chief paymaster for the local steel company. His parents were Russian immigrants, and all he knew was hard work. Big John was rough and tough and a stickler for following the rules. His motto was, "Do the right job, correctly, each time." (Generally that meant doing the job his way.) But Big John was very good at his job, and in his own way he was very lovable.

Well Big John was unhappy with the way the trailers carrying the merchandise to the store were being loaded. It seemed that as the business grew all over the company, the trailers were being just crammed with merchandise. There didn't seem to be any pattern to the way the merchandise was being loaded, and frequently merchandise had been damaged either as it was loaded back in the warehouse or during the trip to the store. The damaged merchandise was double trouble. First, damaged merchandise took more time to handle. Paperwork needed to be completed because it was damaged, and then it had to be handled several times and possibly stored. Second, the merchandise was not available for sale, which impacted sales negatively. Big John took all of this personally.

Big John was constantly complaining to Bill about the situation, but Bill didn't have time to deal with the problem right then. Big John kept complaining, and he knew how to complain. It occurred to Bill that the CEO was coming to the store to hold all employee meetings. Bill told Big John to bring it up during the meeting, and he would support him. Bill knew the CEO loved to hear from the local employees.

The day arrived for the meeting, and Big John didn't open his trailer as usual that morning. He wanted to open it in front of the CEO. Big John told the CEO about the issue with the trailers during the meeting. As Bill predicted, the CEO went back to the receiving area with Big John to open the trailer. What the CEO saw disturbed him greatly. He saw a trailer crammed with merchandise obviously loaded poorly. There was evidence of damaged merchandise, which really frustrated the CEO. And, the trailer was nearly impossible to unload without damaging other things.

The CEO helped Big John and his team unload the trailer that day. The CEO told Big John and his team that he would be back with some help with the next trailer. He told Big John not to touch the trailer until the CEO and his team arrived. Big John didn't know what that meant exactly, but he thought it sounded like a good sign.

The CEO called the VP of distribution and the warehouse manager and told them to wait until he returned to headquarters. When he returned to headquarters he told the VP and warehouse manager that he wanted the two of them plus the people who loaded the trailer for Big John's store to meet him at six o'clock in the morning. They were going for a ride and would be gone all day.

The next morning as they were heading to Big John's store, the CEO told the group that they were going to the store to unload the trailer they had loaded the day before. The CEO thought he heard a collective groan as he finished his statement.

As the trailer door was raised, merchandise began to fall out all over the dock. The trailer was a mess, with damaged merchandise everywhere. The CEO told Big John and his team to get some chairs and watch "the experts" unload the truck. So Big John and his team watched (in amusement) as the CEO, the VP of distribution, the warehouse manager, and the people who loaded the trailer unload the trailer. The CEO took the lead role, crawling into the trailer and making sure to point out all of the poor work. The CEO had made his point to everyone, and in a few weeks all of the trailers for all of the stores were being loaded with care.

The CEO looked at this problem as a breakdown in the company's goal-setting process. He realized his message to get the merchandise to the stores meant the warehouse people were going to find a way to use every inch of trailer space without thinking about damage and the difficulty in unloading the trailer at the store. And the stores, with their sense of urgency to get the merchandise on the sales floor, were going to hurry as they unloaded the trailers, causing more damage.

The CEO got involved, saw the problem, and solved the problem. But more importantly, the CEO showed true leadership by taking ownership of the root cause of this process breakdown.

Did the CEO take the correct approach by getting involved so directly, or should he have had the VP of distribution handle the entire issue?

Was the CEO meddling and micromanaging the entire affair?

After all, there was a VP of operations who could have gotten involved.

What did the CEO's direct involvement mean to the culture of the company?

How did the various and obviously uncoordinated departmental objectives impact the whole situation?

Was the CEO a real leader or a micromanager?

The Tools

Leadership as a concept has been discussed for centuries and has yet to be well defined academically. In practice, it's just as difficult to define because it is so situational in execution. In this Chapter, we've attempted to provide you with "tried and true" leadership concepts that, when put into practice, will help you do your job as a supervisor.

1. Effective "leadership" as a concept has been the subject of hundreds of articles, academic papers, and books. Attempts to "academically" define the subject can be traced back to Frederick Taylor and his studies on "scientific management" in the late 1800s. Yet, among the dozens and dozens of definitions there are some common concepts. We believe that most everyone could agree that effective leadership is the process of guiding and/or directing a group (team) to the successful achievement of a common goal.

2. And a key concept here is one that has also been the subject of many writings—synergy. It's a proven concept in psychology where "two heads *are*, in fact, better than one." People working together, communicating, discussing and debating problem solutions, get better answers than people working alone. *Thus* the leadership principle of teamwork.

3. As an FLS you are the designated leader of your team. You have the *responsibility of creating, managing and maintaining a work* environment where the team goals can be achieved. As the FLS, you will find the need to constantly nurture and build your team to ensure success. The idea, concept, or skill of team building is not always intuitive to everyone, but it can be learned. Many organizations have even adopted a formal leadership/team building program. Nevertheless, there are some basics to team building that we have felt are common to any program.

4. There are two types of teams in the corporate environment:

- The first and most common is the notion of being a

part of the company team. It means the success of your department has a direct impact on part of the company or "big" team. In order for you to maximize your team's impact on company success, your individual goals, your employee's goals, and your team (department) goals must be aligned with and support the broader company goals. It is only possible to maximize company results if all teams have consistent and common goals. The commonality of goals (from the CEO, to all other departments, to the frontline employee) must be clearly established and communicated. And the rewards for success must be consistent as well. Practicing effective communication and enforcing company policies and procedures in an effective manner will support any formal team building program. And, don't forget to recognize the professional achievements (such as working one year, five years, or whatever years without being absent) and personal milestones (a twenty-fifth wedding anniversary or birth of a child) of your team members.

- The second type of team is one that is established separately from the normal departmental structure. This type of team is typically established to attack a specific corporate challenge. Often many of the team members have not worked together in the past. In many cases these types of teams have very specific goals that may not yet be aligned with the company's long-term goals. In these cases, the FLS team-building efforts are different in that they are directed to solving a specific problem.

Tips: **The FLS is the leader of his/her work team and is responsible for creating and maintaining an "open communications" environment. Work with your people by communicating with them and involving them in your processes. You'll wind up with higher productivity-and better answers to your problems.**

A Story

We're familiar with a number of companies and the different styles of their leaders and how their leadership styles drive the culture of the organization. We want to comment about two different styles of leaders that are manifested in two simple leadership gestures. One organization provides parking to its employees in a multilevel parking garage. The parking spaces are not assigned and taken individually each day. Every spot except for one is first come first serve. The CEO's spot is directly next to the door of the building closest to the CEO's office. And that spot is marked in big, bold, black letters: this spot reserved for the CEO (name spelled in big, bold letters). This organization can be best described as a top-down organization, with most of the attention going to the CEO. There is little empowerment here.

We drove to the second organization one day for an early morning meeting with the CEO. The parking lot next to the building was empty, and since we were very early, we parked away from the building and did some work. A few minutes later a car drove into the lot just a few rows away. The occupant struggled to get out of his car—obviously having had some recent surgery. He got his briefcase out of the trunk and started walking to the building. It was the CEO. His name was on the building, and he parked his car, while injured, about as far away from the entrance as possible. The organization had an open culture, creative and free-spirited. They were amazingly successful in a very competitive environment while growing from a local to a global business.

The two leadership styles couldn't be more different. Now, where would you want to work?

Notes

_____

_____

_____

_____

_____

_____

_____

_____

_____

_____

_____

_____

_____

_____

_____

_____

_____

_____

_____

_____

_____

_____

Chapter 10

OCCUPATIONAL SAFETY

The Situation

It was the holiday season. In fact, it was the morning of December 23, the last regular working day before the Christmas holiday. And as usual, everyone was busy trying to get their work completed before rushing off to do their last-minute holiday errands.

Frank started the day as usual for his utility company employer. He held a brief "tailgate" safety meeting. During these meetings he would discuss the previous day's activities and the current day's projects, report on injuries or violations, and mention anything that had occurred throughout the company that was safety related. Normally there was nothing to report, but today was different.

In another part of the state there was a call from a contractor about an underground cut line in a new housing development. Apparently the contractor cut the line early in the day but called just before quitting time to report the line cut. Of course at this time of day, just before the holidays, everyone was in a hurry, just like today.

A crew arrived from a different location to respond to the emergency, and no one had all of the proper repair tools. Being in a hurry, the crew members jumped into action to repair the leak, taking a few shortcuts along the way. These were shortcuts they had taken dozens of times before, all in the name of getting the job done quickly and inexpensively. This time there would be no shortcuts to success. An accident occurred, and several members of the crew were injured. The early investigative reports blamed speed and the inattention to safety procedures for the accident.

Frank took his time relating the incident. In fact, he told the story twice. Of course by now everyone in the company knew about what had happened and their immediate response was, "It won't happen to me. I'm too smart." Frank sensed that no one was paying attention. Everyone was simply too busy to concentrate.

Frank sent his people out to work and hoped for the best. He was very nervous that day for some reason, and, worst of all, he felt helpless.

Woody and his small crew were hoping to finish a job before the holiday break. If they completed their work before 3:00 p.m., then the new homeowners could be in their home before Christmas morning.

Woody was an experienced employee. He was a twenty-five year veteran of the industry and had seen about everything one would see in the field. He was smart, knew the equipment and their limitations, and was generally careful. Or at least he thought he was always careful. Besides, he was experienced and could operate any piece of equipment.

Woody had a solid crew that he managed. Normally there were three members of the crew plus Woody, but today there were only two members since a crew member had taken a vacation day. But even with being short one member, Woody felt they could get the work done before 3:00 p.m. At least Woody thought that before he and his crew had to respond to a midmorning emergency.

Woody and his crew wrapped up the emergency just before lunch and ate their lunch "on the fly." Woody and his crew were determined to finish the work before 3:00 p.m. and without any overtime. Woody knew the boss was watching overtime very closely.

Well, everything was progressing on schedule except it had started to rain. The rain meant that the crew would have to hand rake everything instead of using the equipment. Most of the raking was on a hill, and it wasn't safe to use the tractor. There was a chance the tractor would slide on the wet ground and flip. So Woody and his men jumped on the raking. But after thirty minutes it was clear the work could not be finished on time, and it was beginning to rain a bit harder. Woody decided to take a chance.

Woody knew using the tractor was a calculated risk. He had done it before when he was younger, and there were never any accidents. Woody jumped on the tractor and started raking the hill. The tractor slid down a time or two, but Woody was always able to recover. But his last trip down the hill was different. The tractor began to slide down, and Woody could do nothing to prevent it from rolling over and maybe rolling over on him. Just in the nick of time Woody made a long jump off and hopefully away from the tractor. As he jumped, Woody, while saying a few "Aves," reported later that he was hoping he might just sprain an ankle or break a bone. Either would be better than having the tractor roll over him and likely causing severe injury or death—the normal outcome.

Woody was lucky. He emerged muddy and shaken but free of injury. Once the crew cleared the equipment, they were able to finish the job by hand. Woody had been able to do most of the work on the tractor before the accident. Woody proved once again why he was the crew leader. In fact, the entire crew was very proud of their work. But there was the matter of the damaged equipment and the accident/incident. No one was injured, and there was no lost time. The incident report would be scrutinized a bit, but the entire episode would be overlooked because of the success of the project.

Frank was in his office when he heard the guys talking in the shop. Frank's office was adjacent to the shop, and he could hear every word and didn't like the sound of any of it—his best employee taking chances and working in an unsafe manner. Here was an employee who put his life in danger for a foolish goal. The damage to the equipment, while not insignificant, was the least of his problems. Everyone in the shop was calling Woody a hero, but Frank knew better. And Frank knew that Woody also realized in his heart that he was wrong.

Frank couldn't bring himself to deal with Woody and the accident. Frank knew that everyone was anxious to leave for the holiday break, and this was not the time for any learning to occur. The fact was that Frank did not have the full report from Woody. It would take a few days to sort through the facts. Frank did ask Woody to stay overtime with his crew to get the incident report written as accurately as possible.

While everyone left the office in a good mood, Frank was left with the incident report, which he would digest over the holidays. The problem was, Frank knew the report was going to give him indigestion over the holidays.

What safety environment existed in this company?

There appeared to be some focus on safety, but did the focus really dictate employee awareness and thinking?

What role did Frank's boss play in creating a safe working environment? For that matter, what role does senior management play in establishing a safe working environment?

What advice would you give the company leadership? Any specifics?

What advice would you give Frank? What about Woody?

Are operating costs higher in an unsafe company?

The Tools

In our experience, most organizations misunderstand the importance of occupational safety, treating it as a legal compliance issue rather than an operational issue. Poor management of safety is almost always expensive in terms of human losses, settlement costs, legal issues, lost time and poor execution of work. Organizations with a proactive safety approach have better employee morale, less turnover, and more productive business processes. Proactive management equals improved profitability. By using the tools provided in this Chapter, your organization will make safety an integral part of your business philosophy, thereby reducing costs and improving profits.

1. The subject of safety is a broad one that has evolved into its own profession/field of expertise, but as an FLS you'll have to indelibly print only one overriding factor in your mind—*you* are ultimately responsible for the safety of your employees!

2. Most private employer safety obligations were substantially modified in 1970 by the passage of the Federal Occupational Safety and Health Act (OSHA), which provides for industry specific safety standards—and the general duty to maintain a workplace that is reasonably safe and healthful for employees—free from recognized serious hazards. Some industries are covered by other laws, for example, in mining and transportation.

3. Although US accident frequency and severity rates are in decline, the costs of accidents, over $50 billion a year, are increasing, and state workers' compensation costs are on the rise. Containing these costs is part of your job. It has been our experience that employees who work for an organization that has a strong focus on safety are likely to be more loyal to the company and its mission, have higher morale, and be more productive.

4. Safety standards vary widely by industry (e.g., the construction industry suffers the most fatalities, and their safety-related requirements differ dramatically from other industry standards). FLSs must know the specific standards applicable to their industry/

process/department. *Every employee needs to realize that tripping over an open desk drawer can cause as much damage and injury as a construction accident.*

5. Accident prevention is the *key* in avoiding accidents and injuries. You must *engage* your employees in the prevention process, motivate them to avoid accidents, and assure that they are well trained in their jobs. Postings and signs (Be Safe! Safety is Job #1, etc.) are futile. The key to accident prevention is to get all employees to recognize their individual responsibility for their own safety.

6. Once employees are involved in helping to avoid accidents and have been trained to perform their job efficiently and safely, they need to be motivated. Rewarding employees for good safety performance (individually or as a group) *works*. But don't give out plaques and certificates of merit. Use money (which might be funded through workers' compensation savings) or other meaningful rewards. And it doesn't take a lot—we've been successful in significantly reducing accidents by awarding $50 a year to accident-free employees.

7. As an FLS, you can't be expected to know all the details of OSHA (or the corresponding state requirements) or have expertise in all of the subjects included in a well-run occupational health and safety company program. But you must have familiarity with the various components and requirements as they apply to you. Among others, these include:

- OSHA inspections and employer inspection options (e.g., the right to accompany an inspector)

- OSHA requirements for reporting, postings, and accident notification

- Keeping records of all work-related injuries and illnesses

- Safety requirements for air quality, noise levels, and temperatures in the work environment

- Rules about drug and alcohol use in the workplace

- Ergonomic design of processes and equipment

- Providing well maintained tools and equipment and personal protective equipment (safety glasses, ear protection, safety shoes, gloves where required, etc.)

- Safety training (how to work safely)

- First aid and CPR, etc.

- Hazardous materials and required material safety data sheets

- Safety rules and their enforcement (and corresponding employee discipline)

- Disaster and emergency preparedness and response and, in some cases, providing medical examinations

- Certain employee rights, such as receiving required training, asking OSHA to investigate alleged hazardous conditions, etc.

A Story

Numerous textbooks and guides have been written about occupational safety since the passage of the Occupational Safety and Health Act (OSHA) in 1970.

Thousands of US employees continue to be killed annually in the course of their employment; millions are injured, and many tens of thousands become ill because of chemical/substance exposures. Although OSHA has significantly reduced these figures, the fact remains that too many people are killed, injured, or become ill on the job.

And the FLS is the first line of defense for an employee's safety and welfare on the job.

If the FLS isn't "deadly" serious about enforcing safety rules and regulations, believe me, his/her employees won't be either. And I mean *strict*_enforcement, using, if necessary, progressive discipline. (Enforcement may sometimes anger employees.) In the long run, doing business safely, within the rules, is the only way of doing business, and employees will ultimately respect you for your approach.

Remember, you as the FLS are dealing with your employees' lives and livelihoods. The employer, through you as its agent, is generally *absolutely* liable for injuries on the job (state workers' compensation). You must believe that accidents on the job are generally avoidable (and we have yet to see an *act of God* accident). Eliminating all accidents (and even near misses) will certainly increase your department's productivity, reduce its operating expenses and legal exposures, and, most importantly, eliminate harm to your people.

Notes

Notes

Chapter 11
MANAGEMENT OF YOUR TIME

The Situation

Lewis was excited about his promotion. After ten years of contributing to his employer's success, he was finally going to enjoy the fruits of his hard work. He was being promoted to a supervisory position in the same department where he had worked as a clerk for these many years. Lew's spouse and two grade-school children were proud of him, and Lew was anxiously anticipating the extra money he'd have to spend on the family. Lew's family was the most important thing in his life, and he was grateful that they'd now be able to enjoy some of the things that previously they could not afford. Lew was even planning on starting a college fund for the two kids, something that had been important to him ever since the kids were born.

The job itself was brand new to Lew, and once he got started, he was surprised at all the previously unknown tasks he was now expected to perform. Business was growing quickly for his employer, and Lew's boss apologized that he didn't have the time to properly train and orient Lew. The boss told Lew to do the best he could, and that, given Lew's previous job performance and knowledge of the department, "he was sure to succeed in the new job."

Lew wasn't so sure. He seemed to be picking things up quickly, and he was able to get some help from friends who had been made new supervisors over the last few years, but it sure was taking time. What with coming in early to prepare for the day, coordinating activities with other departments, going to seemingly unending meetings, and talking with his employees, Lew was coming home later and later each day, tired enough to only eat and soon after jump into bed. He figured his eight-hour days had now escalated to eleven or twelve hours, and, to top it off, he had to come in most Saturdays.

Lew was starting to wonder:

Was it worth it?

Could he better balance work and family time?

Was it possible to reduce his daily work hours?

What could he do to improve his productivity, both at work and at home?

The Tools

Managing your time (most frequently inaccurately called time management) is not a subject that many of us learn in school. It's not even a subject taught in most business schools. The subject appears to be relegated to the mysterious teachings of consultant seminars and business books. But it *is* a subject that we need to study because it affects the lives of most of us. Most newly appointed supervisors, in particular, quickly learn: (1) that they are now a Fair Labor Standards Act (FLSA) exempt employee without legal eligibility for time-and-one-half pay for weekly hours worked beyond forty, and (2) they generally, as a supervisor, now have to regularly work more than forty hours a week.

1. Most new supervisors haven't even finished celebrating their promotion when they learn they have to adopt a new set of job rules. No surprise, since in reality they are now in a brand new profession and career.

2. You find out that you now have more money and new prestige, *but* you have a lot to learn, more complicated and expanded job duties, new obligations to communicate with employees and peers, etc., etc. And that all translates to more time on the job—time for your employees, time for your new boss, time for your involvement in the business, and maybe even new time to train or at least meet with other newer supervisors to compare notes.

3. And this additional time requirement could mean that you automatically accept going from a forty-hour workweek to a sixty-or-more-hour workweek. And that will mean serious life changes, even impacting your physical or emotional health and your relationships with spouse and children. Promotions to supervision can mean a life change—but your objective now is to get the job done, and to get it done efficiently, not to restrict yourself to a forty-hour week.

4. A sixty-hour regular workweek doesn't have to be. We *can* manage ourselves and change behaviors to improve our performance of new and varied tasks in the times allotted to us.

How?

Step 1 is documentation.

Keep a daily written diary for at least two weeks to log all tasks that take you ten or fifteen minutes or longer. Log all personal tasks, such as family phone calls or coffee breaks, and business tasks, such as talking with employees, your boss, or other departments, updating e-mail responses or budgets, checking inventory, etc. (After you complete your diary, the subjects in which you "lump" your activities will become more apparent.)

Step 2 is evaluation/analyzation of your diary findings.

Are you surprised at the summary of your diary activities? Get any ideas? Are you spending an hour a day, five hours a week, on personal calls? Are you meeting with employees multiple times on the same subject—maybe indicating the need for a single weekly staff meeting? *Where* are you *wasting* time and *where* can you combine efforts, delegate efforts, or even eliminate efforts?

Step 3 is doing a written plan.

Use your diary analysis and your own personal objectives (e.g., I have to be home with my spouse and kids at least four times a week before 6:30 p.m.) to outline a plan of action which includes a daily calendar of events. This will be a working document, subject to changes and improvements, but if you don't plan your path, you might not reach your destination. Consider incorporating some proven practices in your plan.

Step 4 is evaluating some "best practices."

Everyone is different, and we all have different strengths and weaknesses, but consider some of the following to see if they may work for you:

- Use a proven system like a commercially available diary/ planner or an online software program to help plan, track, and manage your affairs.

- Prioritize—you must accomplish important/urgent tasks first, regardless of your personal feelings or what you're comfortable with. The time proven old prioritization formula still applies. *Do in this order:* (1) important and urgent, (2) important but not urgent, (3) urgent but not important, and (4) not important and not urgent.

- Delegate or eliminate low-priority tasks such as those that are neither important nor urgent.

- Combine activities. Try checking and returning phone messages and e-mails *only* twice a day, maybe first thing in the morning and then after lunch. You don't have to respond to all calls or e-mails—some are informational only (e.g., where you're cc'd or bcc'd on a message). Make sure your computer filters are set up to appropriately screen out (or in) e-mails.

- Ask for help if you need it. Other supervisors or other company experts in accounting or human resources can and will share their expertise. IT experts can help set up and organize computer files, websites and addresses so they are easily accessed and available for storage. And don't be a procrastinator—it'll make things worse, and people don't like to help others with a "last minute, drop everything" problem.

- Do a to-do list of daily priorities and tasks and review/ modify it first thing every morning.

- Try to deal with communications only once. That goes for touching mail or e-mails or phone calls. You may want to devote your twice a day plan to return calls to also dealing with mail (while you're waiting for phone responses). If matters require more thinking or research, include them on your to-do list.

- If at all possible, periodically schedule yourself to work when no one else is there (Saturdays, early mornings).

It's amazing how much you can get done without interruptions.

- Consider utilizing an iPhone or Blackberry. You can access your calls and e-mails and calendar and to-do lists away from your office and not lose valuable time.

- And remember, a trait of many efficient, successful people is choosing what *not* to do (not what to do).

Step 5 is being wary of "problem" employees.

Many supervisors, especially those new to the profession, find that they may be asked to spent significant time with a "few" employees, who appear to need more direct time than other employees. (Sometimes it's more time than the rest of the other employees combined.) These "time demanders" may be well motivated and may enjoy the extra time they spend with the boss, but care must be taken to prioritize your time and let these employees know (in a nice way) that they need to have their issues addressed along with the other employees at your regular staff/departmental meetings.

Another, very different, issue is the true problem employee who may not be performing their job, or may not be following the rules, or may not be coming to work on time (or at all). Significant time may be spent with them—either record keeping, note taking, counseling, or in disciplinary meetings. Regardless of the organization, a minority (generally 5 percent or so) of your people may be "problems" and demand 25 percent of your time. The answer is simple—counsel with them, make sure they know of their inappropriate, unacceptable behavior, use progressive discipline if necessary, and change their behavior. And if this doesn't work (and it won't in all cases), the solution, sorry to say, is discharge. There *are* employees who are in the wrong jobs and would be much happier to be working elsewhere.

A Story

Many successful FLSs and managers spend *way* too much time at work because their "on the job" performance, although high quality, is very inefficient. How many people do you know that use work time to regularly visit with fellow employees, discuss current news topics and family activities, view personal websites, and generally socialize? Some employees we've known may spend three hours every day on these personal matters.

Their employer takes no action, because these people may be very good at what they do—when they do get around to doing it. And the employer pays the same for these FLSA exempt employees. The employee is the one who generally suffers.

Notes

Chapter 12
FUNDAMENTALS

The Tools

Part A: Company (Senior Management) Fundamentals: The (Hopefully Formal) Structure You Need to Run Your Business

Business Plan

This plan would represent the actual roadmap to your building the business. It would include one- and five-year revenue and expense forecasts plus financing requirements. It should include persuasive evidence that a market for the product or service exists and have a study performed on competition and the marketplace.

Value and Performance Model

The V and P model is the direct flow of the strategic and daily operations from the company's mission, vision, values/culture, goals and objectives, and policies and procedures (both official and unofficial) that drive the engine of the business toward optimum success. The visual of this model can be vertical or horizontal, but every element must be linked in a consistent and supportive manner. And the model must be organized in a way to allow routine "audits."

Planning Process

A basic one-year plan and five-year plan (if ready for that) that would include financial goals and budgets should be in place. Also include business goals like market penetration, market share, etc. This would include departmental goals and individual goals. The main emphasis would be on measurable goals and an outline of the "path" of achievement. There would be some structure developed around reporting (example would be monthly, quarterly, etc., actual against budget or plan). This would be a direct input to the PMP (see performance management plan). The formal planning process links the entire organization together in a transparent fashion so everyone can see business results.

Internal Communication Process

This would include scheduled meetings. Topics would include financial reporting, market and competitive analysis reporting, forecasts, and employee issues. These meetings would be supported by various written communication pieces such as all employee e-mails, and formal monthly and quarterly documents. A key point is that all written publications (example would be employee handbook) need to support one another in style and content.

Performance Management Plan

Basically this is a formal employee appraisal process but on steroids. It would include formal reporting against all goals, individual, departmental, and corporate. The process would be transparent, scheduled, and professionally managed (auditable). Peer involvement is critical to success. Remember to link the organization together.

Training Plan

The training plan will be guided by two key drivers, the results of the PMP and the business needs (more specifically, the required skill sets/core competencies and the gap analysis results). The plan needs to be written with measurable goals and objectives. Too many companies train just for training sake. Your training needs to be guided by metrics. Use the market and your competitors to assist you in defining your scope and effort. Don't forget to ensure the individual employee understands and accepts his or her own role in identifying training.

Compensation Plan

The compensation plan should be "pay for performance" driven. The plan should be market based. (Do you want to be a leader, a follower, or competitive?) The plan should be formal, written, and transparent. And it can't be a secret. Effort should be taken to communicate the plan.

Staffing Plan

The staffing plan is originally driven by the business plan, but, like all aspects of your business, it will need constant attention and updating. You will need to address basic questions such as, do we have too many people or too few? Do we have the correct skill sets? You will have to answer even more complicated questions such as, what will the future market trends bring and when should we make adjustments to meet the market demands? Every business must deal with the staffing issues to ensure future success. These issues include both increasing and reducing staffing levels.

One key aspect of your staffing plan is succession planning. Each FLS, manager, director, and executive needs a successor. Identifying a successor is the responsibility of each person in management. The succession plan should be in place to assist in the identification process and to identify any training/development needs of the successor. The notion of developing a succession plan may seem burdensome, but generally the PMP can identify the key employees. Obviously it becomes more complicated as you move up the organization chart. But that is to be expected.

Employment Policies

Most organizations have some form of company employment policies, normally organized and contained in a "handbook," which would also include the ethics policy and fairness doctrine. We urge you to maintain an up-to-date handbook. The handbook, while seemingly routine, is the keystone from which all else is built and communicated. A well kept handbook is the starting point for open communications and business success. A poorly maintained handbook is the starting point for employee confusion, employee dissatisfaction, litigation, and business failure.

Part B: "Everyday" Fundamentals for Supervisors

This is a summary of the key fundamentals for supervisors stated in the book, and it can be used as an everyday guide. It may even be helpful to make a copy of the chapter and keep it in your folder along with your goals and objectives.

1. People are a very important asset of an organization, maybe the most important. The FLS's relationship with his or her own employees is a critical component of business success.

2. The FLS needs to know and understand how the organization makes money and who the company's most important customers are.

3. You need to know your organization's product(s) and what differentiates your company from the competition.

4. As an FLS, you must understand the general accounting principles of "business engagement" in order to communicate effectively with your employees about the company's business objectives.

5. If as an FLS you don't understand the company's value and performance model and possess the ability to articulate it, there is little chance that your employees will understand it.

6. Understand that 90 percent of your employees will agree with 90 percent of the company's business decision, and with your decisions as an FLS if you tell them, in advance, the whats and whys of the decisions.

7. Evaluating employee performance is one of the most difficult if not the most difficult task an FLS (and every person who manages another person) has to do. Identifying and communicating weaknesses in people you work with every day is not easy. Providing this feedback is, however, necessary and a key responsibility of the FLS.

8. As much as practical you, the FLS, must link specific corporate goals and objectives to departmental goals and objectives and then

117

to the daily business activity of the frontline employees. You need to communicate the linkage, and the employees need to understand it.

9. As an FLS you can do everything right with respect to administering compensation and benefits, enforcing uniform company policies, etc., yet, without effective communications and the resulting employee involvement, you will not achieve your business goals.

10. Our experience tells us that one breakdown in the communication link (the ICP) will likely create a potential problem in execution or a missed business opportunity for the organization. Most employee grievances and complaints (as well as most union organizing drives) are a result of a communication breakdown in the immediate relationship between employee and supervisor.

11. The FLS must know when to alert the experts when they might encounter certain issues (such as discrimination allegations) that may have an impact beyond their own department.

12. The FLS must be sure to document any legal issues for possible future reference and be trained to use existing organization forms that are used in the regular course of business. The organization should have these forms readily available.

13. An FLS with union-represented employees must be trained to understand their collective bargaining agreement (CBA) and how to avoid or resolve grievances.

14. As an FLS you are the company designated leader of your team. You have the responsibility of creating, managing, and maintaining a work environment where the team goals can be achieved.

Part C: A Sample Contract of Engagement with Employees

(Organization) intends to promote a leadership position in our industry by growing our business and providing reliable high quality and services in an increasingly competitive environment. Our management and employees need to understand clearly what they are responsible for if we are to achieve this result. The following statement is intended to help in developing that understanding.

Where Our Business Is Now, Is Headed, and Why

Our industry has not always been subject to the extreme competition it now has. The economy has stimulated more customer selectivity, and new financial and market pressures have emerged. We are exposed to more and more emphasis on reducing costs without sacrificing reliability and quality. The old ways of doing business are over. It's happened throughout manufacturing and in the railroad, trucking, airline, utility, and service industries in general. It is now part of our life.

In response to the movement toward cost improvement, restructurings, mergers, and acquisitions have swept industry. Our desire and intent is to remain in control of our destiny as a company. To do so, we'll need to focus on growing, lowering costs, and increasing the value of our client/customers.

Employee expectations are also changing—they generally want more involvement, better communications, more recognition for contributions, and improved market pay and benefits. Addressing these expectations will be part of creating our future business success.

What We Can Do

All Employees

All employees must be responsible for:

- Being at work and working safely

- Performing their jobs efficiently

- Eliminating waste

- Controlling costs

- Contributing to the improvement of the processes and procedures used in their jobs

- Communicating their ideas for improvement to their co-workers and immediate supervisor

- Responding clearly, completely, and honestly when asked for their opinions and ideas

- Improving their skills, learning new skills, and learning about utilizing new technologies to improve their productivity and the quality of their work

- Accepting that there will be more risk in our business in the future than there has been in the past

- Accepting there will never be enough resources to do everything, and work must be done effectively to get the most value for the resources available

Management Employees

Management employees must be responsible for:

- Treating all employees honestly and fairly

- Developing, testing, and implementing processes and new technologies that enable employees to work efficiently, eliminate waste, and control costs

- Providing training and development opportunities to employees who desire to improve their skills, either to perform better in their present jobs or to qualify for other jobs

- Explaining to employees clearly, completely, and honestly how the business is doing, how the employees are doing, and what we know and what we don't know about the present and the future

- Encouraging employee initiatives to improve job performance and work processes, subject, as always, to compliance with regulations and quality standards

- Listening to, evaluating, and responding to employee opinions and ideas

- Recognizing extraordinary contributions by employees

- Designing and implementing an organization structure that focuses everyone on adding value for the customer and shareholder

- Matching employees skills and talents to jobs, coaching them in applying their skills and talents and evaluating their performance regularly and honestly

- Continuing to diversify the work force and treating all people fairly

- Providing qualified employees the opportunity to be considered for other jobs when they become available

- Assisting employees in the transition to other jobs or employment outside the company if changes in business conditions cause their jobs to be eliminated

- Structuring pay and benefits to reflect the marketplace, the effect of increasing competition, individual performance, company success, and the importance of the particular skill or competency to the company's future success

The company believes that the future competitive advantage, success, and growth of our business enterprise are the most important benefits that we can give our employees. This success will result from the creative contributions of all of our people.

SUMMARY

In business management and life in general, there are right and wrong ways to do things. Much of effective management is learned, situational, and impacted by timing. Over our years of experience, we have been exposed to (and we've executed) many mistaken management tactics and strategies. We still believe there are basic management principles that are timeless and effective. In this book we've attempted to present many of these principles as practical tools for frontline supervisors and their bosses.

Our use of stories and business examples is meant to provide an interesting environment for supervisors to reflect on fundamental concepts in real world situations. Hopefully FLS's will consider these concepts and tools in helping them achieve improvements in the people part of their businesses.

Closing Notes

_____

_____

_____

_____

_____

_____

_____

_____

_____

_____

_____

_____

_____

_____

_____

_____

_____

_____

_____

_____

_____

Closing Notes

_____

_____

_____

_____

_____

_____

_____

_____

_____

_____

_____

_____

_____

_____

_____

_____

_____

_____

_____

_____

Closing Notes

_____

_____

_____

_____

_____

_____

_____

_____

_____

_____

_____

_____

_____

_____

_____

_____

_____

_____

_____

_____

Closing Notes

_____

_____

_____

_____

_____

_____

_____

_____

_____

_____

_____

_____

_____

_____

_____

_____

_____

_____

ABOUT THE AUTHORS

TOM ZABOR and **TIM HEWITT** are experienced business practitioners who have served as officers/executives of prominent public companies.

Tom has engineering and law degrees, and, in addition to his executive management experience, has practiced law for a large national employment/labor law firm. Tim has been the President of several organizations, and has an MBA from a "top tier" business school. They've worked side by side for over twenty years and have together learned life lessons about the successful supervision of people.

Tom and Tim are both married with adult children, and have a consulting/training practice in Indiana.